Modern Curriculum Press
BEGINNING
TO
READ
Series

Little Quack

Published by Modern Curriculum Press, Inc
13900 Prospect Road, Cleveland, Ohio 44136

Library of Congress Catalog Card Number: 61-8810

ISBN 0-8136-5544-7 (paperback)
ISBN 0-8136-5044-5 (hardbound)

456789   92 91

Little

Quack

MODERN CURRICULUM PRESS
Cleveland • Toronto

Three little ducks lived in a barnyard.

One hot summer day they went for a
swim.

It was a long way to the lake from
the barnyard.

"I will go first," said Blacky.

"I am not afraid."

"I will go next," said Jacky.

"I am not afraid of anything."

6

"Little Quack must walk behind,"
said Blacky and Jacky.

"He is afraid of everything."

Little Quack did not want to
walk behind.

But he did not say anything.

So out of the barnyard went the
three little ducks.

Blacky was first,

Jacky next,

and Little Quack last of all.

Soon they came to some apple trees.

"Zoom, zoom, zoom!"

"What was that?" cried Blacky.

"An airplane!" cried Jacky.

Blacky hid behind a water can.

Jacky jumped into an apple box.

Little Quack looked up.

"I should like to see an airplane,"
he said.

Little Quack did not see an airplane.

But he did see a big fat bumblebee.

It was black and yellow.

The bumblebee flew into a pink apple blossom.

"Come out, Blacky!" said Little Quack.

"Come out, Jacky!

That was only a big fat bumblebee."

Blacky came from behind the water can.

Jacky jumped out of the apple box.

"Ha, ha, ha!" they said.

"We knew it was a bumblebee all the time."

Then the three little ducks went on.

Soon they came to a meadow.

They saw some baby rabbits in a nest.

A friendly black and white cow was eating grass.

But the three little ducks did not stop to talk.

Before long the three ducks came
to the lake.

Splash! In went Blacky.

Splash! That was Jacky.

Splash! In went Little Quack,
last of all.

The three little ducks swam in
the water.

They swam around and around.

They pushed the water behind them
with their feet.

"Brum! Brum! Brum!"

"What was that?" cried Blacky.

"Someone beating a drum!" cried Jacky.

Down went Blacky, head first,
under the water.

Down went Jacky, too.

"I should like to see someone
beating a drum," said Little Quack.
He swam over to some tall grass.

18

Jump! Splash!

A big green bullfrog jumped out of the grass.

He swam a little way under water.

Then Little Quack saw him sitting on a log.

"Brum! Brum! Brum!" said the bullfrog.

Then he swam away.

"Come up, Blacky!" said Little Quack.

"Come up, Jacky!

That was only a big green bullfrog."

So up came Blacky.

Up came Jacky, too.

"Ha, ha, ha!" they said.

"We knew it was a bullfrog all the time."

Around and around swam Blacky,
Jacky, and Little Quack.

Down they went again and again,
heads down, tails up.

They looked all around under the water.

They saw some fish.

They saw many pretty stones.

They saw many things that ducks like
to eat.

The three little ducks ate and ate
and ate.

At last it was time to go home.

"We will go home a new way,"
said Blacky.

"We will go home through the garden."

"Old Pussy Cat may be there,"
said Little Quack.

"Ha, ha, ha!" laughed Blacky
and Jacky.

"Who is afraid of Old Pussy Cat?"

Little Quack did not say anything.

Soon they came to the garden.

Oh! Oh!

There was Old Pussy Cat!

But Old Pussy Cat did not see the ducks.

She was looking at a bird.

Blacky hid behind a big cabbage.

Jacky ran behind some flowers.

But Little Quack went up behind
Old Pussy Cat.

He was as quiet as can be.

Old Pussy Cat did not know
Little Quack was there.

Then, snip! He caught hold of the tip
of her tail.

"Meow!"

Away went Old Pussy Cat as fast as she
could go!

"Ha, ha, ha!" laughed Blacky and Jacky.

"Just see Old Pussy Cat go!

Little Quack, you are not afraid of anything.

You must not walk behind us.

We will walk behind you!"

Then back to the barnyard went the
three little ducks.

Blacky was last,

and Jacky next,

and Little Quack first of all.

LITTLE QUACK

Little Quack has a total vocabulary of 170 words. Regular plurals (*-s*) and regular verb forms (*-s, -ed, -ing*) of words already on the list are not listed separately, but the endings are given in parentheses after the words.

5	three		swim		said		and
	little		it		Blacky		he
	ducks		was		am		is
	lived		long		not		everything
	in		way		afraid		did
	a		to		next		want
	barnyard		the		Jacky		but
	one		lake		of		say
	hot		from		anything	**8**	so
	summer						out
	day	**6**	I	**7**	Quack		last
	they		will		must		all
	went		go		walk		
	for		first		behind	**9**	soon

came
some
apple
trees
zoom
what
that
cried
an
airplane

10 hid
water
can
jump(ed)
into
box
look(ed)(ing)
up
should
like
see

11 big
fat
bumblebee
black
yellow
flew
pink
blossom

12 come
only

ha
we
knew
time

13 then
on
meadow
saw
baby
rabbits
nest
friendly
white
cow
eat(ing)
grass
stop
talk

14 before
splash

15 swam
around
pushed
them
with
their
feet

16 brum
Indian
beating

drum

17 down
head(s)
under
too

18 over
tall

19 green
bullfrog
him
sitting
log
away

21 again
tail(s)

22 fish
many
pretty
stones
things
ate

23 at
home
new
through
garden
old
Pussy

cat
may
be
there
laughed
who

24 oh
she
bird

25 cabbage
ran
flowers

26 as
quiet
know

27 snip
caught
hold
tip
her
meow
fast
could

28 just
you
are
us

29 back

31

Margaret Hillert, author and poet, has written many books for young readers. She is a former first-grade teacher and lives in Birmingham, Michigan.